Elvis Presley

CONTENTS

HOW TO USE THE CD ACCOMPANIMENT:

THE CD IS PLAYABLE ON ANY CD PLAYER, AND IS ALSO ENHANCED SO MAC AND PC USERS CAN ADJUST THE RECORDING TO ANY TEMPO WITHOUT CHANGING THE PITCH.

A MELODY CUE APPEARS ON THE RIGHT CHANNEL ONLY. IF YOUR CD PLAYER HAS A BALANCE ADJUSTMENT, YOU CAN ADJUST THE VOLUME OF THE MELODY BY TURNING DOWN THE RIGHT CHANNEL.

ISBN 978-1-4234-6697-0

HAL•LEONARD®
CORPORATION
7777 W. BLUEMOUND RD. P.O. BOX 13819 MILWAUKEE, WI 53213

Visit Hal Leonard Online at
www.halleonard.com

◆ ALL SHOOK UP

TROMBONE

Words and Music by OTIS BLACKWELL
and ELVIS PRESLEY

❷ BLUE SUEDE SHOES

Words and Music by
CARL LEE PERKINS

TROMBONE

3

❸ CAN'T HELP FALLING IN LOVE

TROMBONE

Words and Music by GEORGE DAVID WEISS,
HUGO PERETTI and LUIGI CREATORE

◆ 4 DON'T BE CRUEL
(To a Heart That's True)

TROMBONE

Words and Music by OTIS BLACKWELL
and ELVIS PRESLEY

◆₅ HOUND DOG

TROMBONE

Words and Music by JERRY LEIBER
and MIKE STOLLER

◆ I WANT YOU, I NEED YOU, I LOVE YOU

TROMBONE

Words and Music by MAURICE MYSELS
and IRA KOSLOFF

7 IT'S NOW OR NEVER

Words and Music by AARON SCHROEDER
and WALLY GOLD

TROMBONE

◆ JAILHOUSE ROCK

TROMBONE

Words and Music by JERRY LEIBER
and MIKE STOLLER

◆⑨ LOVE ME

TROMBONE

Words and Music by JERRY LEIBER
and MIKE STOLLER

 LOVE ME TENDER

TROBONE is shown as:

TROMBONE

Words and Music by ELVIS PRESLEY
and VERA MATSON

Slowly, with feeling

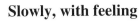

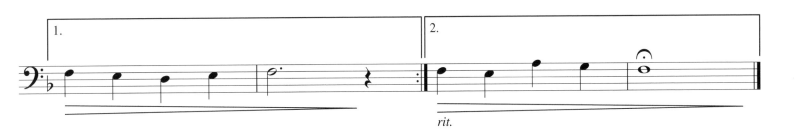

✦ LOVING YOU

TROMBONE

Words and Music by JERRY LEIBER
and MIKE STOLLER

◆12 RETURN TO SENDER

TROMBONE

Words and Music by OTIS BLACKWELL
and WINFIELD SCOTT

⓭ (LET ME BE YOUR) TEDDY BEAR

TROMBONE

Words and Music by KAL MANN
and BERNIE LOWE

◆ TOO MUCH

TROMBONE

Words and Music by LEE ROSENBERG
and BERNARD WEINMAN

◆ WEAR MY RING AROUND YOUR NECK

TROMBONE

Words and Music by BERT CARROLL
and RUSSELL MOODY